Thinking Out Loud

Amy Mitchell

Presentation by *BookLeaf Publishing*

Web: www.bookleafpub.com

E-mail: info@bookleafpub.com

ISBN: 9789357449335

First edition 2023

This book is for my sister Megan.

*Every story I've told or poem I've written
all started by wanting to make you smile
with a tale whilst walking around garden
centres on boring Sunday afternoons.*

ACKNOWLEDGEMENT

I'd like to thank all of my friends and family who encouraged me to write these poems and complete this personal challenge. In particular, my friend Tasha, who completed the Charlotte Bronte challenge with me (we may not have written our poems together, but it kept me going knowing you were writing too).

I'd like to thank my teachers for always believing that I could be an author of some kind, and I'd like to also acknowledge and thank the teachers I work with now, who have helped improve my grammar and vocabulary through relentless English training!

Thank you to my Great Uncle Derek for sharing your own poetry with me. You told me all those years ago that I could be a poet one day too- you were right!

I'd like to thank and acknowledge those close to me that supported me through the months that leading up to and during the time I wrote these poems: Ruth, Elaine, Evie, Sara, Hannah, Amy, Chris, Beth, Dan, Luke, Mum, Jason, Dad and Lyndsey. June- August 2022 were not the brightest months for me, but I wrote these poems anyway and made it through because of all of you. (Even if you didn't realise you were helping, you were).

Finally, thank you to Bookleaf Publishing for making this all possible for me.

PREFACE

This small books of poems were written as part of the Charlotte Bronte Award. I had 21 days to write 21 poems.

The poems in this book may seem random and disconnected- because they are! They are disconnected as each day is from the one that came before. I was in a different mood each time I wrote a poem. I wrote them at different times of day and in different places. Sometimes I would write several poems on a Monday and none at all on a Thursday.
So yes, the poems are disconnected and mismatched, because they are my random inner thoughts for that moment; my catharsis for that hour; my relaxation for that day.

Relentless Questions

Miss Mitchell can I have...?
Miss Mitchell can I ask...?
Miss Mitchell can I go...?

Yes of course you can!

Miss Mitchell can I have...?
Miss Mitchell can I ask...?
Miss Mitchell can I go...?

Yes, once we've done this.

Miss Mitchell can I have...?
Miss Mitchell can I ask...?
Miss Mitchell can I go...?

I'll come to you in a minute.

Miss Mitchell can I have...?
Miss Mitchell can I ask...?
Miss Mitchell can I go...?

Not right now.

Miss Mitchell can I have...?

Miss Mitchell can I ask...?
Miss Mitchell can I go...?

No.

Next September:

Miss Mitchell can I have...?
Miss Mitchell can I ask...?
Miss Mitchell can I go...?

Yes of course you can!

If Beth Were a Bat

If Beth were a bat
She'd wear a funky hat
And fly up to the sky
Oh so very high

If Beth only ate fruit
She'd very rarely toot
As she hung upside down
With her wings above her crown

If Beth were a bat
I think she'd fancy that
Not a vampire, no not scary
But like a friendly Northern fairy

All-Inclusive

Sunshine on the tarmac
Blast of air from the wings
Excitement walking down the stairs
Thinking of what the week brings

Luggage round in circles
Journey to your temporary house
Unpacking all your summer clothes
Skirt, bikini, blouse

Lie-ins till 9
Then rushing down to eat
Drinks from noon-midnight
Holiday-makers to meet

Day trips to the town
Or maybe to the zoo
Dips in the pool together
Then an evening meal for two

A week of luxury living
Forgetting the dreary grey
Sadness when packing up
Shopping on the final day

Raining on the tarmac
Blast of air from the wings
Tired walking down the stairs
Thinking of what the week brings

Lent

The first day was full of hope,
For the achievement that was yet to come.
A few days of continuous fasting,
Never wanting some.

A week of constant bragging,
And praise for the challenge ahead.
Lording over the others,
Who don't worry 'bout what they are fed.

By day 10 the cravings kick in,
The loss is feeling quite strong.
Regretting the awful decision;
Deciding the sacrifice was wrong.

There may be a slip up in week 2,
Or possibly held off til 3.
But no one will know my secret,
That is kept between God and me.

Now a whole month has come to pass,
The pink candle is already lit,
Just 10 more days to go,
I'm happy that I could commit.

The final week of longing,
The time is almost here.
Soon I can break down the barriers,
The finish line- oh so near!

Finally it's Easter Morning,
Church mass is over and done.
The hunger pains can now be answered,
As we've seen the rise of God's son.

Parallel

Driving round and round
Round.
Round.

No space can be found
Found.
Found.

Oh no- there's none!
What do I do?

No simple drive in,
No calm,easy bay.

It's real..
It's happening!

The panic has struck,
The passers by watch.

I have to….

Parallel park!

My Mate Spike

My mate Spike
Rides his bike
Over to Beachy Head

When he gets there
He sits in his chair
At least that's what he said

I always did ponder
Why he doesn't go yonder
And explore past the chalky peak

But one day he told me
He'd never leave by the sea
He hates how northerners speak

Acceptable in the 80s

Dancing in Rio
Purple rain
Expressing yourself
Asking for Fame

Feeling the heat with somebody
Living forever
Moonwalking
Gettin it on together

Falling freely
Dancing in the dark
Girls having fun
A tainted love spark

The 80s era was iconic
And when the 90s began
It really was the end of the world as we know it

Denying Death

I've handled a knife
I've contemplated meth
I've tightened the rope
But I've still denied death

I've taken the pills
I've suffocated my breath
I've walked in the road
But I've still denied death

I've dreamt of these endings
And have even begun
But at the last moment
Death doesn't come

The world's shortest blues song

Da-da-da-dum
Didn't wake up this morning
Da-da-da-dum

Holidaying without my partner

Holding back the tears as I leave you
Only gone for a week, I know
Longing to be home; anticipating the break
Incapable of expressing my sadness
Don't want to be away without you
Any time apart just kills
Yet the break will do me good
So I go, but I'll return

Primary Stage

They come to us at only 4
Barely able to walk through the door
Their parents cling to the doorframe and cry
We urge them just to say goodbye

Come 5 they're ready to read and write
The school day brings so much delight
They laugh and play without a worry
The year goes by in such a hurry

At 6 they prepare to take a test
They hardly seem to get their rest
With phonics, maths and even spelling
We notice them really begin aging

In their 7th year they ask the questions
And start the upper school preparations
They make music, art and compete in sports
Really they just do all sorts

By 8 they've really come into their own
And gosh how tall they've grown
Their times tables are almost recited
And now reading often gets them excited

9 is a time for pre-teen angst
Play fighting and pulling pranks
Then they enter their penultimate year
And parents and child begin to fear

Once their 10, they're ready for the end
They begin to revise; their minds do bend
They prepare for the SATs and other things
And wonder what secondary brings

11 has hit- no one is ready
It wasn't that long since they snuggled their
teddy
They wave us goodbye and sign their shirts
A new class will come- but the leaving always
hurts

The White Oak Gateway

The white oak stands tall
The grooves engraved so finitely
Metal piercing it's middle
Willing to be turned again and again

The nails in the coffin hinge it in place
Swinging the carcass to and fro
The gateway opens for all who will it
Some knock, but some simply just enter

The Himalayas- a renga poem

The Himalayas,
Largest mountain range around,
Wide like a canyon.

Snow-capped peaks all around you,
Unlickable iced sugar!

Five Asian countries:
India, Bhutan, Nepal,
China, Pakistan.

It's one hundred peaks- many!
Kashmir's pride, Asia's wonder!

Tiger

Covered in lightning strikes of orange and black,
Amber eyes alert and ready to attack!
Paws pad softly through the grass and sand,
As silent as a thief prowling across the land.

At first, each step is steady and slow,
Winding through the trees, knowing where to
go,
Ears prick up, the tiger's lips turn up in a smile,
Quick as a flash he reaches his prey, that'll fill
him for a while.

Swoosh, so swift, the tiger is truly and amazing
sight,
I wish I could see a tiger, I wish with all my
might.
Beauty and grace combined into something so
strong,
When will I see a tiger, I hope it won't be long.

Bexhill limerick

There once was a man from Bexhill,
Who took an unusual pill,
It made him turn green,
But also quite lean,
As he became rather seriously ill.

Marley

There once lived Marley the princess,
Who was very hard to impress,
Her high expectations,
Spread throughout the nations,
Yet princes wooed her nevertheless.

Our Love

Seasons come and go,
Sunshine, rain and snow.
But nothing stays with me,
Quite like our loving flow.

The rain will still fall,
The sunshine will call,
But you will still come,
Love me forever and all.

Rainbows will fade,
Tornadoes barricade,
Yet on and on we fight,
Our future ready-made.

Four best friends

Four best friends,
So differently placed in life,
Yet their smiles are frozen in time together,
Through the photo of a memory shared.

Four best friends,
Two living with their partners,
Loved in all possible ways,
But still having love to share with the others.

Four best friends,
One seeking fame and reward,
Wanting a life far better than her own,
Although loving her friends all the same.

Four best friends,
The final one constantly wondering,
Will her smile remain once the photo is take ?
Yes- because she has her best friends.

7 days

Monday- oh joyous day- the union of family friends!
Tuesday- adventurous- visiting London zoo!
Wednesday- new beginnings- gym and pool and spa.
Thursday- solitary- my peaceful day.
Friday- so much fun- wine and dine through the night.
Saturday- flashback- partying in the 80s
Sunday- God's day- rest and plan for it to begin again.

Typical families

Families always bicker.
It's hard to find a reason why.
The calmness is rarely lengthy.
The conversation often dry.

Families always suffer.
Pain can be caused so much.
Sometimes by verbal disagreements.
Sometimes by physical touch.

Families always forgive.
The crying will eventually end.
Yet sometimes they're hard to cope with.
Which is why you also need a friend.

Amy 1 and Amy 2

Amy 1 and Amy 2,
Met when they were young,
Amy 1 told Amy 2,
"I am Amy 1!"

Amy 2 agreed with this,
And enjoyed having a friend,
For she knew Amy 1,
Would always be right in the end.

Amy 1 and Amy 2,
Spent years in fits of laughter,
And they knew they always had,
Each other to look after.

Amy 2 told Amy 1,
"You're like my sister"
And Amy 1 smiled,
As she knew they'd be friends forever!